WINTER WEED FINDER

Identifying Dry Plants of Central and Eastern North America

DORCAS S. MILLER
illustrated by **ELLEN AMENDOLARA**

Nature Study Guild Publishers
an imprint of AdventureKEEN

START HERE

- Review the terms, opposite, and the keys that follow.

- Find typical structures on the plant you want to identify.

- Choose the description that best matches your plant. If it falls into two categories, use the first place it appears in this list:

  Key to distinctive features: Vines; plants with barbs or spines, umbels, opposite branching; plants with small, distinctive fruiting structures or other notable characteristics, p. 2–3.

  Area covered by this book

  Key to structure with one to five or more chambers; how the structure opens to release seeds is also important, p. 4.

  Key to dried flowers: The flower has dried in place; it looks like a flower (or some part of one), p. 5.

- At the key, choose the matching illustration and text, and proceed to the specified page/s.

- Range: For many species, range (R) is throughout (TH). Range may be given as a fraction: n. ½ = northern half of the range map. If the species grows in a portion of the state, the entire state is considered to be in the range. Standard state abbreviations have been used; Que = Quebec; NB = New Brunswick.

© 2024, 1989 Dorcas S. Miller (text) and Ellen Amendolara (illustrations) • ISBN 978-0-912550-53-4
- Printed in China • Cataloging-in-Publication data is available from the Library of Congress
- naturestudy.com

ABBREVIATIONS AND GLOSSARY

p. Page or pages   **H** Height   **x ¾** Illustration ¾ life size   **spp** More than one species

Alternate Leaves, branches, or fruiting structures do not grow opposite each other.

Bracts Modified leaves, found at the base of a flower head; see p. 50.

Burr A dry fruit with hooks that adhere to clothing or fur.

Calyx Outer circle of flower parts (sepals), which in some plants forms a papery covering around a capsule.

Capsule A dry fruit that splits open into two or more chambers.

Head Generally, a dense cluster of flowers or seeds; specifically, used for stalkless or nearly stalkless flowers of the Aster family and some members of the Pea family.

Opposite Leaves, branches, or fruiting structures grow opposite each other at a node.

Pod Generally, a dry fruit that opens; specifically, used for pea pods, which have one chamber and fully open along two seams.

Sharp A dry fruit with straight-tipped prickles, thorns, or spines.

Silique, silicle A two-chambered fruit with translucent partition; specific to the Mustard family; see p. 42.

Whorled More than two leaves, branches, or fruiting structures encircle the stem.

Plants or structures with distinctive features. *Illustrations are examples, not all possibilities*

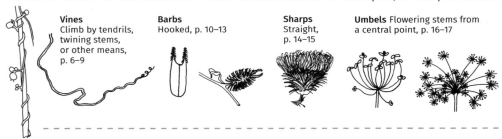

Vines
Climb by tendrils, twining stems, or other means, p. 6–9

Barbs
Hooked, p. 10–13

Sharps
Straight, p. 14–15

Umbels Flowering stems from a central point, p. 16–17

Opposite or whorled branching: *Round stem*

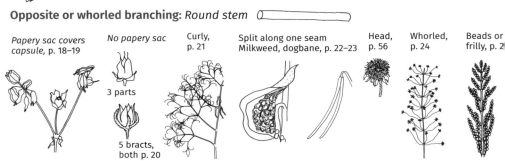

Papery sac covers capsule, p. 18–19

No papery sac

3 parts

5 bracts, both p. 20

Curly, p. 21

Split along one seam
Milkweed, dogbane, p. 22–23

Head, p. 56

Whorled, p. 24

Beads or frilly, p. 2

Opposite branching: *Square stem*

Papery calyx holds seeds, p. 26–29

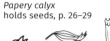

Fruiting structures *crowd stem*, p. 30–31

Stiff capsule holds seeds, p. 32–33

Capped Cup, Bell, Bead, Box, Heart
All less than 0.5" long

Cup and cap, p. 34 *Bell,* p. 34

Bead, p. 35

Box, p. 35

Heart, p. 35

Extended Style, Papery Sac, Three-winged Seed, Head of Seeds

5 vertical panels around *central column,* p. 36

Papery sac covers capsule, p. 37; also see p. 18–19, 25

Three-winged seeds, p. 38

Tightly packed seeds, long hairs, p. 39

Fruiting structure a container with one or more chambers

ONE
Opens by side slits:
Orchid family,
p. 40

One seam
leaves alternate,
p. 22

Two seams
Pea family, p. 41

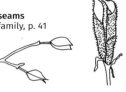

TWO
Silique or silicle,
p. 42–43

Capsules, p. 44

THREE
p. 45–47

FOUR
p. 21

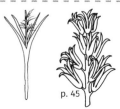

p. 45

FIVE
p. 48–49

**MORE THAN
FIVE** p. 49

Dried flowers or small bushy heads

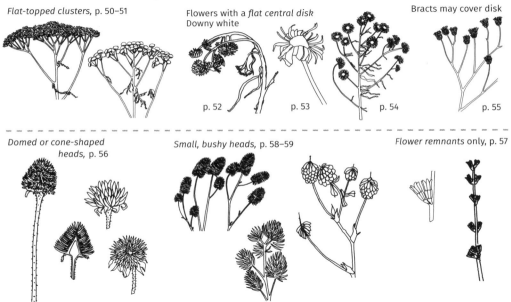

Flat-topped clusters, p. 50–51

Flowers with a *flat central disk*
Downy white

p. 52 p. 53 p. 54

Bracts may cover disk

p. 55

Domed or cone-shaped heads, p. 56

Small, bushy heads, p. 58–59

Flower remnants only, p. 57

VINES
Climbing by tendrils

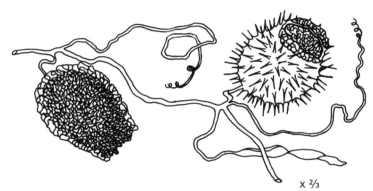

x ⅔

Wild cucumber
Echinocystis lobata
Inflated papery sac with weak spines covering a small luffa (a fibrous sponge) with 2–3 chambers and seeds; in Gourd family, it is the plant that produces bath luffas.
R n. ½

Climbing by twining leaf stems

Vetch, *Vicia* spp;
Vetchling, *Lathyrus* spp
Fruit a pod (1 compartment that splits along 2 seams); typically, the 2 halves curl into spirals.   R TH

(Other pea species, p. 13, 41)

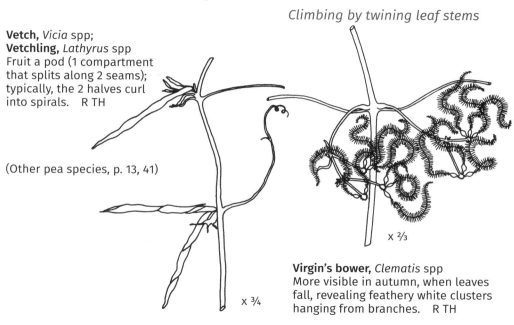

x ⅔

x ¾

Virgin's bower, *Clematis* spp
More visible in autumn, when leaves fall, revealing feathery white clusters hanging from branches.   R TH

8

Climbing by twining stems

Dodder, *Cuscuta* spp
Capsules round, smaller than 0.25" diameter, often clustered; plant a parasite (no green leaves). For other bead-like structures, see sensitive fern, p. 25, and moth mullein, p. 35.   R TH

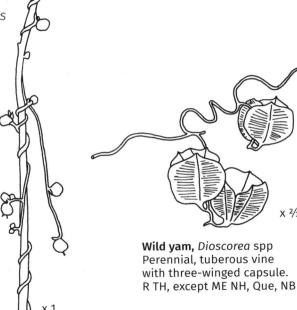

x 2/3

x 1

Wild yam, *Dioscorea* spp
Perennial, tuberous vine with three-winged capsule.
R TH, except ME NH, Que, NB

Hops, *Humulus lupulus*
Perennial with a cluster of enlarged
papery structures, each with fruit inside.
R TH, except Gulf Coast

x ½

Black swallowwort
Vincetoxicum nigrum
Cynanchum louiseae
Fruit, a follicle, full of seeds
with white parachutes.
In Milkweed family, p. 22–23
R n. ½, except IA

x ⅔

BARBS

Enchanter's nightshade
Circaea canadensis
Pear-shaped, entirely
covered with barbs;
H 27" [–39"]   R TH, except FL

Agrimony
Agrominia spp
Nodding, shaped like
a top with one end
covered with tiny, stiff
barbs; H 1–5'
R TH

x 2½

x 1

x 2½

x ⅔

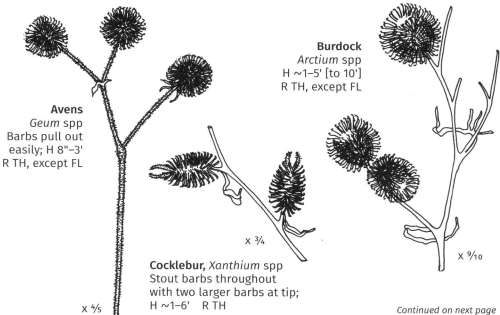

Avens
Geum spp
Barbs pull out
easily; H 8"–3'
R TH, except FL

x ⅘

Cocklebur, *Xanthium* spp
Stout barbs throughout
with two larger barbs at tip;
H ~1–6'   R TH

x ¾

Burdock
Arctium spp
H ~1–5' [to 10']
R TH, except FL

x 9/10

Continued on next page

BARBS (continued)

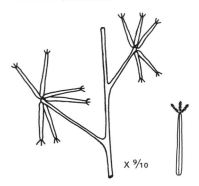

X ⁹⁄₁₀

Spanish needles
Bidens bipinnata
The point of each needle is tipped with
backward-facing spines. There are many
Bidens species, each with its own version
of the "stick-tight" design. H 1–5.6'   R IA–NY s.

X ⁹⁄₁₀

Beggar-ticks
Bidens spp
H 4"–6.6'   R TH

X ³⁄₅

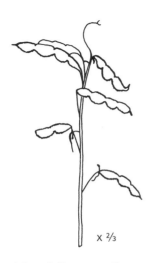

x ⅔

Teasel, *Dipsacus* spp
Egg-shaped; each spine with a
barb at the tip; brought from
Europe for use in making wool
cloth; H 1.6–6.6'   R TH, except
LA, FL, GA, NB

x ⅗

Tick trefoil, *Desmodium* spp
Hooked hairs; breaks apart between seeds
(in segments to 0.5") rather than opening
along two seams, like other species in the
Pea family (p. 41); H 4"–6.6'   R TH

SHARPS

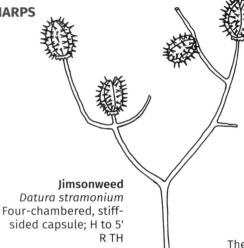

Thistle, *Cirsium* spp
Base of bristles supports
tightly packed long white
strands/hairs; H 8–20",
two species 3.3–11'   R TH

Jimsonweed
Datura stramonium
Four-chambered, stiff-
sided capsule; H to 5'
R TH

The female goldfinch uses this
down, in part, to line her nest.

x ¼

x ⅔–1⅓

The seeds of both **sweet cicely** and **Queen Anne's lace** stick to clothing; see umbels, p. 17.

Wild cucumber, a vine, has weak spines on the exterior, p. 6.

Common viper's bugloss
Echium vulgare
Don't touch! Entire plant is covered with sharp, white spines; H 1–2.6'   R TH, except AL, FL

x ¼–⅓

UMBELS: Flowering stems grow from a central point.

Simple umbels
Each flowering stalk is tipped with a three-parted capsule that houses small, round black seeds.

Wild leek
Allium tricoccum
Capsule deeply 3-lobed;
H 6–10"   R TH, except AR,
LA, MI, FL, SC

x ¼

Wild garlic
A. vineale
Often form only ovoid bulbets
(small bulbs at the tip of the
stalk); flowers, if present,
produce barely lobed capsules;
H 11–35"   R TH, except MN, NB

x ¾

Compound umbels
Each flower stem in the main
umbel is tipped with an umbel.

x ½

Wild parsnip
Pastinaca sativa
H to 4'   R TH, except
AL, MS, FL, GA

Hairy sweet cicely
Osmorhiza claytonii
H 1–3'   R TH, except
LA, MS, FL

x ½

Queen Anne's lace
Daucus carota
Dry umbel shrinks
over time; H to 5'
R TH

x ½

OPPOSITE BRANCHING, round stem, *calyx* covers capsule

Pink family (these two pages)
Stems swollen at joint;
capsule opens by teeth
(often 6, maybe 8 or 10);
1–3 chambers

In Pinks, the *calyx (the combined outer ring of the floral parts)* forms a papery sac enclosing the capsule.

Campion/catchfly
Silene spp
Capsule opens by 8 or 10
teeth; H 4"–6.6'   R TH

Bladder campion
Silene latifolia
Most species
open by 10
teeth; H 8–22"
R TH, except LA,
MS, FL

x ⅔

x ⅘

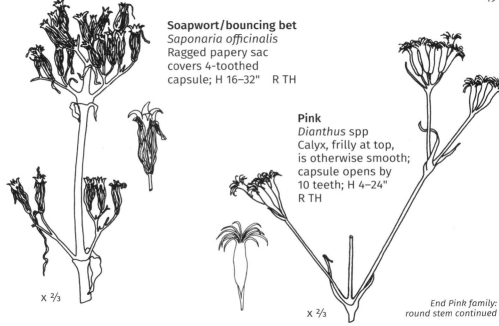

Soapwort/bouncing bet
Saponaria officinalis
Ragged papery sac
covers 4-toothed
capsule; H 16–32"   R TH

Pink
Dianthus spp
Calyx, frilly at top,
is otherwise smooth;
capsule opens by
10 teeth; H 4–24"
R TH

X ²⁄₃

X ²⁄₃

*End Pink family:
round stem continued*

OPPOSITE BRANCHING, round stem,
no calyx covering capsule

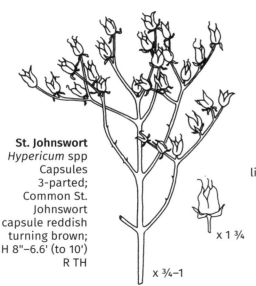

St. Johnswort
Hypericum spp
Capsules
3-parted;
Common St.
Johnswort
capsule reddish
turning brown;
H 8"–6.6' (to 10')
R TH

x 1 ¾

x ¾–1

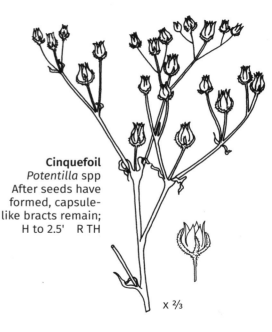

Cinquefoil
Potentilla spp
After seeds have
formed, capsule-
like bracts remain;
H to 2.5'   R TH

x ⅔

Willow-herb
Chamerison spp
Often branched; capsule
slender; 4 side panels
open from central column,
releasing tiny seeds, each
with a halo of white hairs;
after release, panels curl into
a mass of frills; H to 6.6'
R TH, except AL, FL

Fireweed/great willow-herb
Chamerion angustifolium
Single stalk; capsules on upper section
of stalk; plant often plentiful after fire;
H 3–10' R n. ½

x ¼

*Opposite branching,
round stem continued*

OPPOSITE BRANCHING*, round stem,
follicles (split open along one seam)

Milkweed family
Follicles grow in pairs.
Seeds tipped with long white
hairs for wind dispersal. (Black
swallowwort, a vine, p. 9, is also
in the Milkweed family.)

* Butterfly milkweed, *Asclepias
tuberosa,* has alternate leaves.

Milkweed
Asclepias spp
Follicles warty, 2–5" long;
H to 6.5'
R TH, except AR, LA, MS

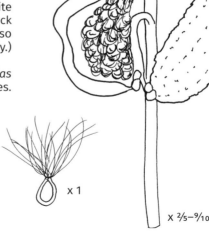

x 1

x ²/₅–⁹/₁₀

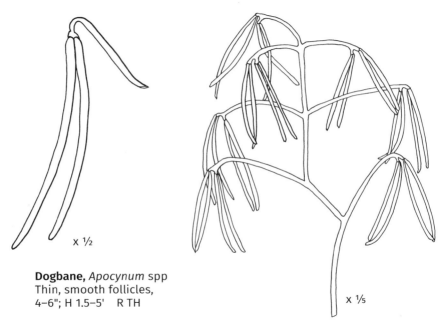

x ½

Dogbane, *Apocynum* spp
Thin, smooth follicles,
4–6"; H 1.5–5'   R TH

x ⅕

OPPOSITE BRANCHING, round stem,
flowers whorled around the stem

Whorled loosestrife
Lysimachia quadrifolia
5-part capsule, one per flower
stalk; 4 (sometimes 3 or 5) stalks
whorled around stem; plant
usually unbranched; H 12–40"
R TH, except LA, MS, FL, SC;
NH–VT–ME n.

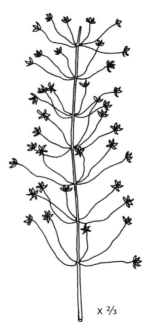

x ⅔

Plants with rows of beads
or frilly structures

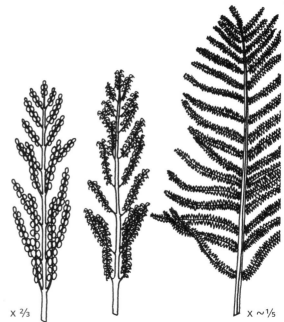

Fertile fronds: Lined with small,
bead-like containers that burst
open, releasing spores.

Sensitive fern (left, middle)
Onoclea sensibilis
Fertile frond (near right), beads
opened (center and above).
Common in wet sites, low
woods, and other areas; spore-
bearing frond persists through
winter; H 10–16"   R TH

Ostrich fern (right)
Matteuccia struthiopteris
Found along waterways, floodplains,
rich woods; H 12–29"   R n. ½

x ⅔

x ~⅕

OPPOSITE BRANCHING, square stem,
papery calyx

Mint family: Square stem
usual (twirl between
thumb and index finger);
fruiting structures
whorled around stem or
at tip of flowering stem

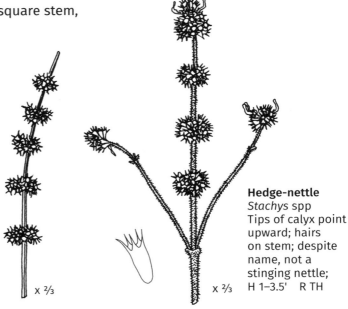

Motherwort
Leonurus cardiaca
Calyx 5-pointed, flaring;
no hairs on stem; H 1.3–5'
R TH, except FL

x ⅔

Hedge-nettle
Stachys spp
Tips of calyx point
upward; hairs
on stem; despite
name, not a
stinging nettle;
H 1–3.5'   R TH

x ⅔

Water horehound
Lycopus spp
Parts too small
to distinguish by
eye; H to 39"
R TH

Pennyroyal (left)
*Hedeoma
pulegioides*
Calyx 2-lipped,
3 teeth above,
2 below; H 4–16"
R TH, except LA, FL

Self-heal (right)
Prunella vulgaris
Upturned, toothed,
hairy, petal-like
bracts; H 4–20"
R TH

x ⅔   x 1   x ¾   *Mint family
continued*

28

Bergamot/bee balm
Monarda spp
Tiny, narrow calyxes radiate from central point at tip of stem; H 1–5'   R TH

Field mint
Mentha arvensis
Calyxes grow from small branches at tip of fruiting stalk; H 8–32"
R TH, except s–e.

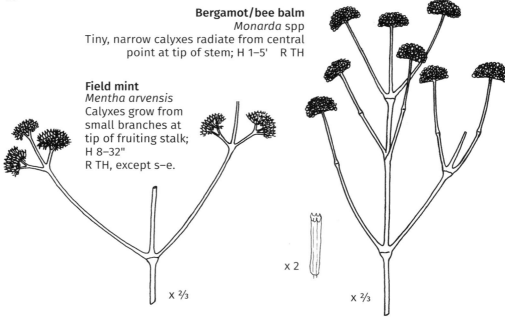

x ⅔

x 2

x ⅔

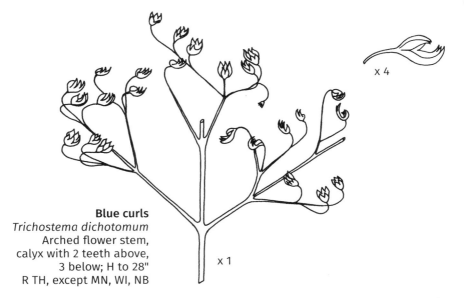

x 4

Blue curls
Trichostema dichotomum
Arched flower stem,
calyx with 2 teeth above,
3 below; H to 28"
R TH, except MN, WI, NB

x 1

End Mint family
Continue to opposite branching, square stem

OPPOSITE BRANCHING, square stem, *flowers or remains crowd upper branches*

Purple loosestrife
Lythrum salicaria
2-parted capsule covered by flower remains; found in wet areas (rivers, lakeshores, ditches, wetlands); H 4–6'
R TH, except LA, FL, SC
Very invasive

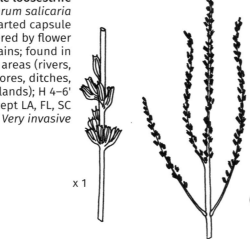

x 1

Vervain
Verbena spp
Papery calyx with 4 teeth; H to 6"
(a few species 3–8')
R TH

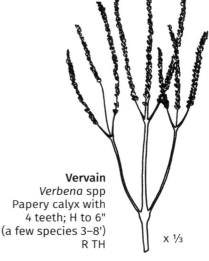

x ⅓

OPPOSITE BRANCHING, square stem,
2-chambered capsules
Capsules crowd upper stem

x 2

Turtlehead
Chelone glabra
Capsule white; spherical; wet
woods and other damp areas;
H to 3.5'   R TH, except LA, FL

x ½–¾

2-chambered capsules continued

OPPOSITE BRANCHING,
square stem,
*2-chambered
capsules*

x 2

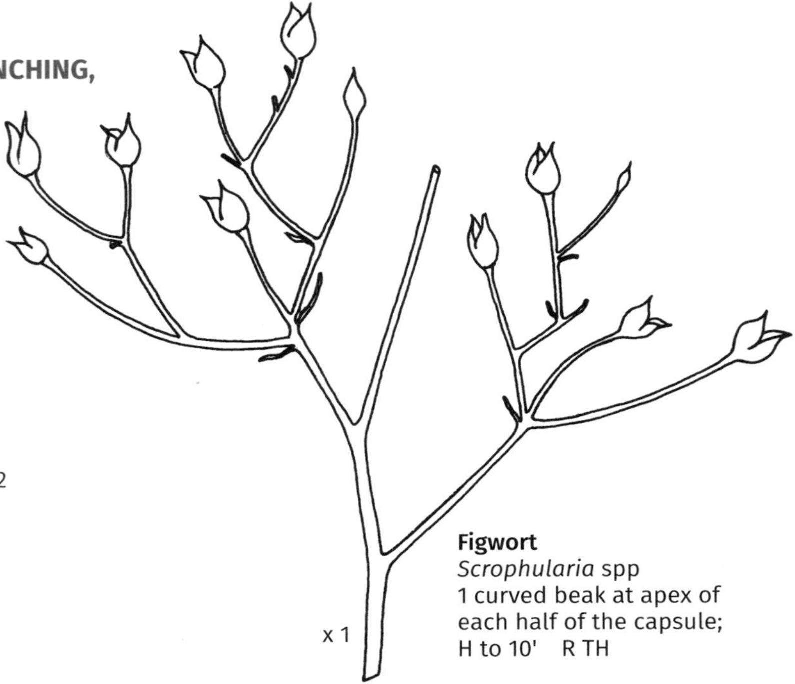

x 1

Figwort
Scrophularia spp
1 curved beak at apex of
each half of the capsule;
H to 10'   R TH

Capsule length

Figwort	0.25–0.36"
Beardtongue	0.25–0.5"
False foxglove	0.5–0.75"

False foxglove
Aureolaria spp
1 curved beak at apex
of each half of the
capsule; H 1.5–6.5'
R TH, except Que, NB

x 1

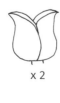

x 2

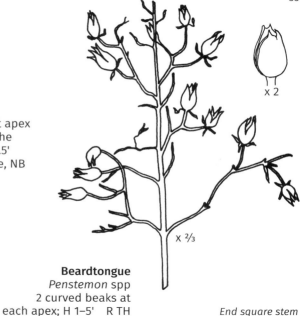

x 2

x ⅔

Beardtongue
Penstemon spp
2 curved beaks at
each apex; H 1–5'   R TH

End square stem

34

SMALL SEED CONTAINERS

Containers less than 0.5" long
Cone, bell (p. 34), bead, cube, heart (p. 35)

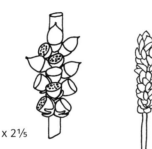

x 2⅕

Cone-shaped cap pops off, allowing seeds to spill from base.

English plantain
Plantago lanceolata
Capsules at top of
stem; H 6–16"   R TH

Common plantain
P. major
Capsules along ⅔ of stem;
H 2–12"   R TH

x ½   x ½

Bellflower
Campanula spp
Nodding, bell-like capsule;
H 1.3–3.3'
(for tall bellflower, 1.6–6.5')
R TH, except AR, LA, MS

x ⅔

Bead
Moth mullein
Verbascum blattaria
Capsule splits into 2
chambers; H to 5'   R TH
(For other beads, see
p. 8, 25.)

Cube
Seedbox/square-pod
Ludwigia alternifolia
Capsule opens by
terminal pore;
4 chambers; H 1–4'
R TH, except MN, VT, NH,
ME, Que, NB

Heart-shaped, flattish
2-parted capsule

Common speedwell
Veronica arvensis
H 2–5"; other plants
in genus, 2–4", except
long-leaved to 3'
R GA–IA n.

For tiny circle of 5
follicles, see p. 48.

x ⅔

x 1

x ⅓

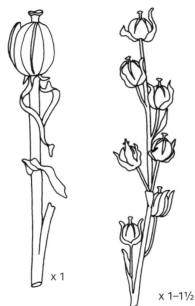

x 1

x 1–1½

EXTENDED CENTRAL COLUMN,
surrounded by 4 or 5 chambers

*(Left) Plants have no chlorophyll;
capsule white or—when dry—black;
flowers nod, then turn upward*

One-flowered ghost pipe (far left)
Monotropa uniflora
Single flower; H 4–12"   R TH

Pinesap
Hypotiys spp (near left)
Capsules alternate on stem; H 4–12"
R TH

Shinleaf (right)
Moneses spp
Plant has chlorophyll; dry
capsule brown; 5-chambered
capsules nod; H 4–8"   R IA–VA n.

x 1

Enclosed in a papery sac

Wild tobacco
Lobelia inflata
Calyx roundish,
0.4" diameter; H to 40"
R TH, except FL

Other plants with
papery exterior:
Pink family, p. 18–19

Ground cherry
Physalis spp
Heart-shaped with 5 or 10 veins
running from base to point;
structure 0.8–1.6" long.
Chinese lantern, a garden plant
that sometimes escapes,
has a 2"-long red calyx; H 8–35"
R TH

x ⅔

x ⅔

x ⅔

Three-winged seeds

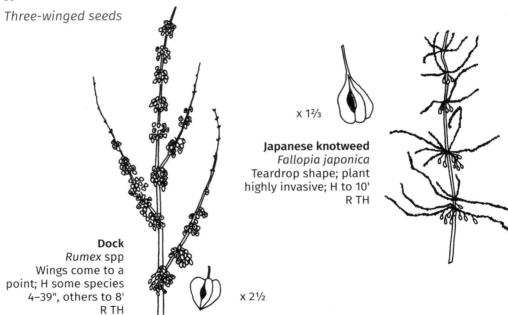

x 1²/₃

Japanese knotweed
Fallopia japonica
Teardrop shape; plant
highly invasive; H to 10'
R TH

Dock
Rumex spp
Wings come to a
point; H some species
4–39", others to 8'
R TH

x 2½

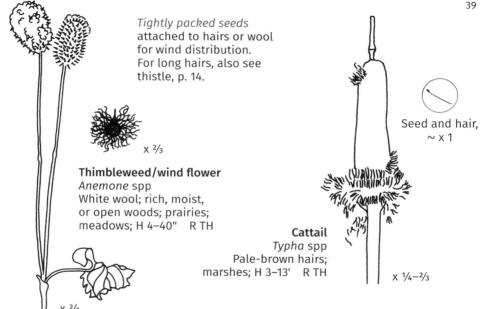

Tightly packed seeds attached to hairs or wool for wind distribution. For long hairs, also see thistle, p. 14.

Thimbleweed/wind flower
Anemone spp
White wool; rich, moist, or open woods; prairies; meadows; H 4–40"   R TH

x 2/3

x 2/3

Seed and hair, ~ x 1

Cattail
Typha spp
Pale-brown hairs; marshes; H 3–13'   R TH

x 1/4–2/3

End of Distinctive Features

FRUITING STRUCTURE WITH ONE OR MORE CHAMBERS
One chamber, opens by slits: Orchid family

x 1

Broad-leaved helleborine
Epipactis helleborine
Capsule with 3 slits, 0.4–0.6"
long; widespread. In some
areas, considered aggressive;
H to 32"   R TH, except LA–SC

Downy rattlesnake plantain
Goodyera pubescens
Capsule ~0.25" long with 3 slits;
H 8–16"   R TH, except LA

x ¾

Lady's slipper
Cypripedium spp
Capsule with 6 slits;
1–2" long; H 4–32"
R TH, except FL

x ⅘

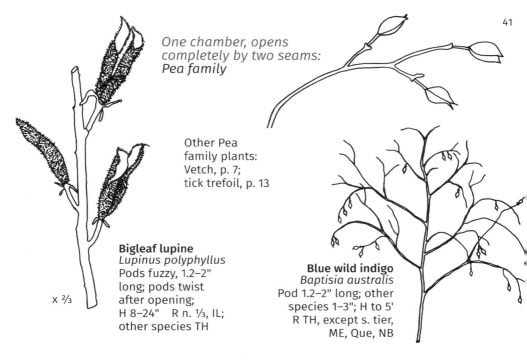

One chamber, opens completely by two seams: Pea family

Other Pea family plants: Vetch, p. 7; tick trefoil, p. 13

Bigleaf lupine
Lupinus polyphyllus
Pods fuzzy, 1.2–2" long; pods twist after opening; H 8–24"   R n. ⅓, IL; other species TH

x ⅔

Blue wild indigo
Baptisia australis
Pod 1.2–2" long; other species 1–3"; H to 5' R TH, except s. tier, ME, Que, NB

42

Two chambers separated by translucent partition: Mustards

Silique: Length longer than width
Silicle: Length and width similar

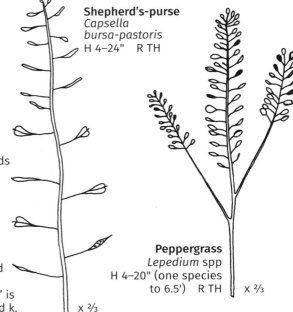

a. Silique intact.
b. Exterior drops away, revealing seeds and translucent partition.
c. Seeds drop away, leaving only translucent partition.
d. Partition drops away, leaving only skeletal outline.

Pronunciation
Silique: Two syllables with the second pronounced "leek."
Silicle: Three syllables; the second "i" is short, the "c" is pronounced as a hard k.

Shepherd's-purse
Capsella bursa-pastoris
H 4–24"   R TH

Peppergrass
Lepedium spp
H 4–20" (one species to 6.5')   R TH

x ⅔

x ⅔

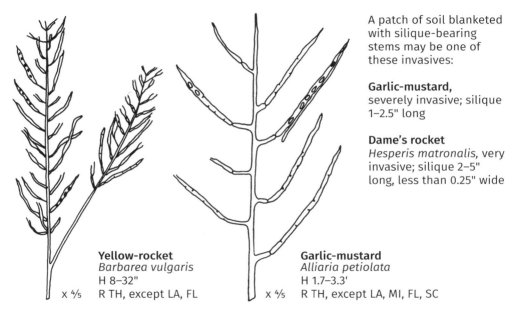

A patch of soil blanketed with silique-bearing stems may be one of these invasives:

Garlic-mustard, severely invasive; silique 1–2.5" long

Dame's rocket *Hesperis matronalis,* very invasive; silique 2–5" long, less than 0.25" wide

Yellow-rocket
Barbarea vulgaris
H 8–32"
x ⅘   R TH, except LA, FL

Garlic-mustard
Alliaria petiolata
H 1.7–3.3'
x ⅘   R TH, except LA, MI, FL, SC

Two chambers separated by an opaque partition

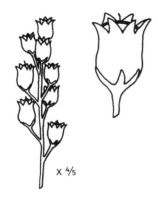

X ⅘

Common mullein
Verbascum thapsus
Structures tightly packed
along upper portion of
stem; stem and leaves
covered with soft, fuzzy
hairs; H to 6.6'   R TH

Butter-and-eggs
Linaria vulgaris
Urn-shaped; opens by 6 to 8 teeth at the top
of the capsule; inner partition easily visible; H 1–2.6'   R TH

X ⅓

Three chambers, capsule smaller than ⅛" long
Three chambers continued next page

Four chambers

Common evening primrose
Oenothera biennis
Lobes peel back from
central column; capsule
1–1.5"; capsules located
terminally or at node,
where leaf joins stem;
H 2–6'   R TH

x ½

Pinweed
Lechea spp
H 4–32"   R TH

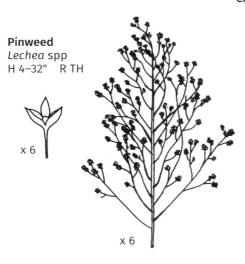

x 6

x 6

Fireweed and **Willow-herb**, p. 21,
also in Evening Primrose family,
have 4-parted capsules that curl
to the base and appear frilly.

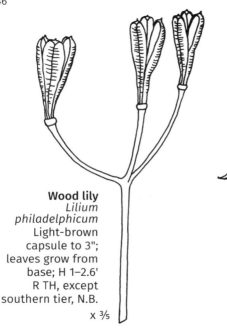

Capsule with three chambers
Wood lily, yucca, blue flag:
Flat black seeds form in two stacks per chamber.

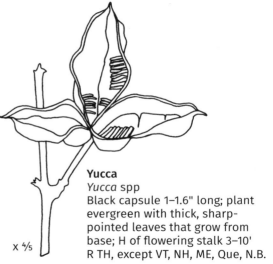

Wood lily
*Lilium
philadelphicum*
Light-brown
capsule to 3";
leaves grow from
base; H 1–2.6'
R TH, except
southern tier, N.B.

x ³⁄₅

Yucca
Yucca spp
Black capsule 1–1.6" long; plant
evergreen with thick, sharp-
pointed leaves that grow from
base; H of flowering stalk 3–10'
R TH, except VT, NH, ME, Que, N.B.

x ⁴⁄₅

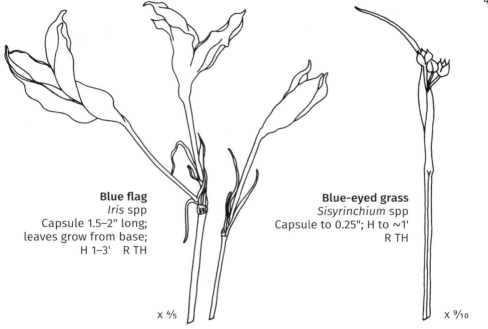

Blue flag
Iris spp
Capsule 1.5–2" long;
leaves grow from base;
H 1–3'   R TH

Blue-eyed grass
Sisyrinchium spp
Capsule to 0.25"; H to ~1'
R TH

X ⁴⁄₅

X ⁹⁄₁₀

48

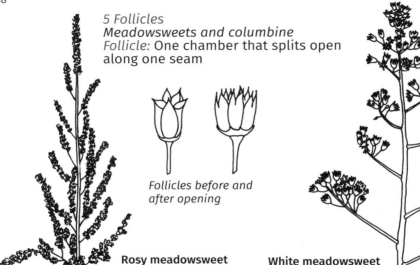

5 Follicles
Meadowsweets and columbine
Follicle: One chamber that splits open along one seam

Follicles before and after opening

Rosy meadowsweet
Spiraea tomentosa
Flower cluster narrow;
H to 4'
R TH, except AL, FL, IA

x ⅓

White meadowsweet
S. alba
Flower cluster
broader; H to 6.5'
R MO, TN, NC n.

x ⅔

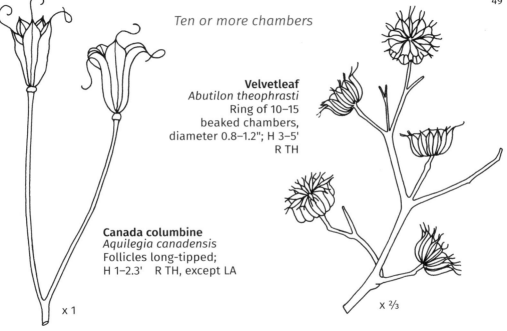

Ten or more chambers

Velvetleaf
Abutilon theophrasti
Ring of 10–15
beaked chambers,
diameter 0.8–1.2"; H 3–5'
R TH

Canada columbine
Aquilegia canadensis
Follicles long-tipped;
H 1–2.3'   R TH, except LA

x 1

x ⅔

DRIED FLOWERS AND FLOWER PARTS

These pages illustrate members of the Aster family, which is characterized by a cluster of modified flowers. Also, instead of the usual outer floral ring (the sepals) below the petals, these plants have leaf-like bracts below the flower head.

Disk flower

Ray flower

Bract

x ⅔

Yarrow
Achillea millefolium
Tan bracts; H 8–39"
R TH

Flower types	Examples	
Both ray and disk	Aster, sunflower	Seeds may disperse by floating; latching on to fur, hair, or clothing; being eaten by birds or mammals; or other means.
Ray only	Dandelion	Seeds disperse quickly by various means.
Disk only	Tansy	Concentration of seeds; may resemble a button.

Flat-topped flower clusters

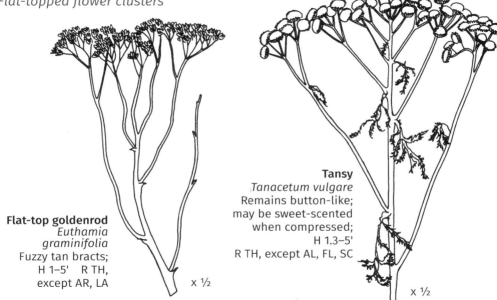

Flat-top goldenrod
*Euthamia
graminifolia*
Fuzzy tan bracts;
H 1–5'   R TH,
except AR, LA

x ½

Tansy
Tanacetum vulgare
Remains button-like;
may be sweet-scented
when compressed;
H 1.3–5'
R TH, except AL, FL, SC

x ½

Flowers with a flat central disk

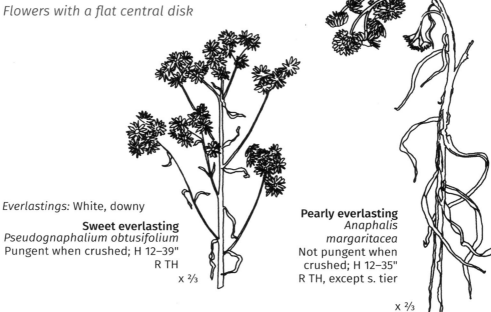

Everlastings: White, downy

Sweet everlasting
Pseudognaphalium obtusifolium
Pungent when crushed; H 12–39"
R TH
x ⅔

Pearly everlasting
*Anaphalis
margaritacea*
Not pungent when
crushed; H 12–35"
R TH, except s. tier

x ⅔

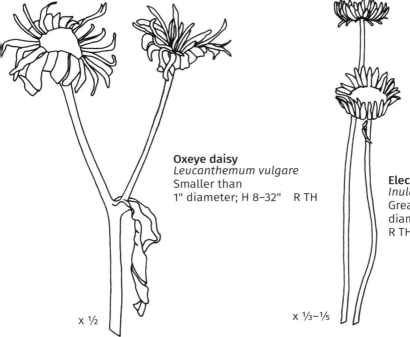

Oxeye daisy
Leucanthemum vulgare
Smaller than
1" diameter; H 8–32"   R TH

Elecampane
Inula helenium
Greater than 1"
diameter; H 6.5'
R TH, except s. tier

x ½

x ⅓–⅕

Continued

Aster
Symphyotrichum spp
Bloom in late summer and fall,
so post-bloom structures
younger than those of plants
that bloom in early summer;
H 1–4' usual, with
some species smaller
and some to 6.5'   R TH

X ⅓–⅔

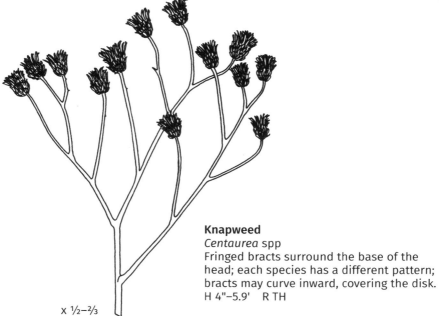

Knapweed
Centaurea spp
Fringed bracts surround the base of the
head; each species has a different pattern;
bracts may curve inward, covering the disk.
H 4"–5.9'   R TH

x ½–⅔

Head in which bracts form a cone-shaped, rounded, or curved-in surface

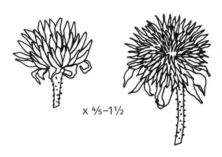

x ⅘–1½

Sunflower
Helianthus spp
Flower heads solitary on long stalk;
plants with either alternate or opposite branching;
H to 10' (in one species, to 13')   R TH

Coneflower
Rudbeckia spp
H 1–6.5'   R TH

x 1

No head, just remaining bracts

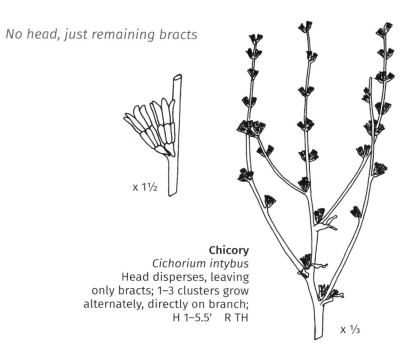

x 1½

Chicory
Cichorium intybus
Head disperses, leaving
only bracts; 1–3 clusters grow
alternately, directly on branch;
H 1–5.5'   R TH

x ⅓

Structures small, bushy,
composed of dried calyxes,
each with a tiny pod

Low hop clover
Trifolium spp
Drooping, petal-like calyxes
reminiscent of hops, p. 9;
H 4–20"   R TH

x ⅔

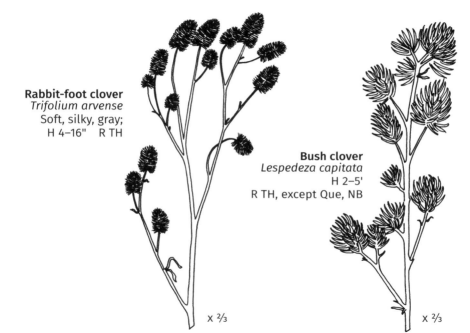

Rabbit-foot clover
Trifolium arvense
Soft, silky, gray;
H 4–16"   R TH

Bush clover
Lespedeza capitata
H 2–5'
R TH, except Que, NB

x ⅔

x ⅔

INDEX

Abutilon theophrasti, 49
Achillea millifolium, 50
Aureolaria, 33
Agrimony, *Agrimonia*, 10
Alliaria petiolata, 43
Allium tricoccum, vineale, 16
Anaphalis margaritacea, 52
Anemone, *Anemone*, 39
Apocynum, 23
Aquilegia canadensis, 49
Arctium, 11
Asclepias, 22
Aster, 54
Avens, 11
Baptisia australis, 41
Barbarea vulgaris, 43
Beardtongue, 33
Bee Balm, 28
Beggar-ticks, 12
Bellflower, 34
Bergamot, 28
Bidens, 12
Blue curls, 29
Blue flag, 47
Blue-eyed grass, 47

Bouncing bet, 19
Burdock, 11
Butter-and-eggs, 44
Campanula, 34
Campion/catchfly, 18
Capsella, 42
Cattail, 39
Centaurea, 55
Chamerison, 21
Chelone glabra, 31
Chicory, 57
Cichorium intybus, 57
Cinquefoil, 20
Circaea lutetiana, 10
Cirsium, 14
Clematis, 7
Clover, 58–59
Cocklebur, 11
Columbine, 49
Coneflower, 56
Cucumber, wild, 6
Cuscuta, 8
Cypripedium, 40
Daisy, oxeye, 53
Datura stramonium, 14

Daucus carota, 17
Desmodium, 13
Dianthus, 19
Dioscoria, 8
Dipsacus, 13
Dock, 38
Dodder, 8
Dogbane, 23
Echinocystis lobata, 6
Echium vulgare, 15
Elecampane, 53
Enchanter's nightshade, 10
Epipactis helleborine, 40
Euthamia graminifolia, 51
Evening primrose, 45
Everlasting, 52
Fallopia japonica, 38
Fern, sensitive, ostrich, 25
Figwort, 32
Fireweed, 21
Foxglove, false, 33
Garlic, field, 16
Garlic-mustard, 43
Geum, 11
Ghost pipe, 36

Goldenrod, 51
Goodyera pubescens, 40
Ground cherry, 37
Hairy sweet cicely, 17
Hedeoma, 27
Hedge-nettle, 26
Helianthus, 56
Helleborine, broad-leaved, 40
Hesperis matronalis, 43
Hops, 9
Humulus lupulus, 9
Horehound, water, 27
Hypericum, 20
Hypopitys, 36
Indigo, blue wild, 41
Inula helenium, 53
Iris, 47
Jimsonweed, 14
Knapweed, 55
Knotweed, Japanese, 38
Lady's slipper, 40
Lathyrus, 7
Lechia, 45
Leek, wild, 16
Leonurus cardiaca, 26

Lepedium, 42
Lespedeza capitata, 59
Leucanthemum vulgare, 53
Lily, wood, 46
Lilium philadelphium, 46
Linaria vulgaris, 44
Lobelia inflata, 37
Loosestrife, purple, 30
Loosestrife, whorled, 24
Ludwigia alternifolia, 35
Lupine, bigleaf, 41
Lupinus polyphyllus, 41
Lycopus, 27
Lysimachia quadrifolia, 24
Lythrum salicaria, 30
Matteuccia struthiopteris, 25
Meadowsweet, 48
Mentha, 28
Milkweed, 22
Mint, field, 28
Monarda, *Monarda*, 28
Monesis, 36
Monotropa uniflora, 36
Motherwort, 26

Mullein, common, 44
Mullein, moth, 35
Mustard, 42–43
Nightshade, enchanter's, 10
Oenothera biennis, 45
Onoclea sensibilis, 25
Osmoriza claytonii, 17
Parsnip, wild, 17
Pastinaca sativa, 17
Pennyroyal, 27
Penstemon, 33
Peppergrass, 42
Physalis, 39
Pinesap, 36
Pinks, 19
Pinweed, 45
Plantain, *Plantago*, 34
Plantain,
  downy rattlesnake, 40
Potentilla, 20
Prunella vulgaris, 27
Pseudognaphalium, 52
Queen Anne's lace, 17
Rudbeckia, 56
Rumex, 38

St. Johnswort, 20
Saponaria officinalis, 19
Scrophularia, 32
Seedbox, 35
Self-heal, 27
Sensitive fern, 25
Shepherd's purse, 42
Shinleaf, 36
Silene, 18
Sisyrinchium, 47
Soapwort, common, 19
Spanish needles, 12
Speedwell, common, 35
Spiraea, 48
Square-pod, 35
Stachys, 26
Sunflower, 56
Symphyotrichum, 54
Swallowwort, black, 9
Tansy, 51
Tanacetum vulgare, 51
Teasel, 13
Thimbleweed, 39
Thistle, 14

Tick trefoil, 13
Trichostema dichotomum, 29
Trifolium, 58–59
Tobacco, wild, 37
Turtlehead, 31
Typha, 39
Velvetleaf, 49
Verbascum blattaria, 35
Verbascum thapsis, 44
Verbena, 30
Veronica arvensis, 35
Vervain, 30
Vetch, Vetchling, 7
Vicia, 7
Vincetoxicum nigrum, 9
Viper's bugloss, 15
Virgin's bower, 7
Willow-herb, 21
Wind flower, 39
Xanthium, 11
Yam, wild, 8
Yarrow, 50
Yellow-rocket, 43
Yucca, *Yucca*, 46

Other books in the pocket-size *Finder* series:

FOR US AND CANADA EAST OF THE ROCKIES

Berry Finder native plants with fleshy fruits
Bird Finder frequently seen birds
Bird Nest Finder aboveground nests
Fern Finder native ferns of the Midwest and Northeast
Flower Finder spring wildflowers and flower families
Life on Intertidal Rocks organisms of the North Atlantic Coast
Scat Finder mammal scat

Track Finder mammal tracks and footprints
Tree Finder native and common introduced trees
Winter Tree Finder leafless winter trees

FOR STARGAZERS

Constellation Finder patterns in the night sky and star stories

FOR FORAGERS

Mushroom Finder fungi of North America

Dorcas S. Miller, founding president of the Maine Master Naturalist Program, has written more than a dozen books, including *Track Finder, Scat Finder, Berry Finder, Bird Nest Finder*, and *Constellation Finder*. Her *Finder* books have sold more than half a million copies.

NATURE STUDY GUIDES are published by AdventureKEEN, 2204 1st Ave. S., Suite 102, Birmingham, AL 35233; 800-678-7006; naturestudy.com. See shop.adventurewithkeen.com for our full line of nature and outdoor activity guides by ADVENTURE PUBLICATIONS, MENASHA RIDGE PRESS, and WILDERNESS PRESS, including many guides for birding, wildflowers, rocks, and trees, plus regional and national parks, hiking, camping, backpacking, and more.